My lover spoke to me & said, Arise my darling, & come with me...

My Heart—
Christ's HOME

Presented to

Sharon, with love,
Cindy

New, Expanded Edition

Published 1989 by Meridian, Grand Rapids, MI 49546
Reprinted 1996 by Meridian, Grand Rapids, MI 49546

M0333 Paperback Gift Edition
ISBN 1-56570-033-3

Manufactured in the United States of America

*I*n his letter to the Ephesians, Paul writes these words: "That [God] may grant you to be strengthened in your inner being with power through his Spirit, and that Christ may dwell in your hearts through faith" (Eph 3:16-17). Or, as another has translated, "That Christ may settle down and be at home in your hearts by faith" (Weymouth).

Without question one of the most remarkable Christian doctrines is that Jesus Christ himself through the Holy Spirit will actually enter a heart, settle down and be at home there. Christ will live in any human heart that welcomes him.

He said to his disciples, "Those who love me will keep my word, and my Father will love them, and we will come to them and make our home with them" (Jn 14:23). But he was also telling them that he was soon to leave them (Jn 13:33). It was difficult for them to understand what he was saying. How was it possible for him both to leave them and make his home with them at the same time?

It is interesting that Jesus uses a similar concept here (home) that he uses earlier in John 14: "I go to prepare a place for you...that where I am, you may be also" (vv. 2-3). He was promising that just as he was going to heaven to prepare a place for them and would one day welcome them there, so it would be possible for them to prepare a place for him in their hearts now. He would come and make his home with them right here.

This was beyond their comprehension. How could it be?

Then came Pentecost. The Spirit of the living Christ was given to the church and they experienced what he had foretold. Now they understood. God did not dwell in Herod's Temple in Jerusalem — nor in any temple made with hands! Now, through the miracle of the outpoured Spirit, God would dwell in human hearts. The body of the believer had become the temple of the living God and the human heart the home of Jesus Christ. Thirty minutes after Pentecost the disciples knew more about Jesus than they had known in the three years previously.

It is difficult for me to think of a higher privilege than to make for Christ a home in my heart, to welcome, to serve, to please and to know him there.

I will never forget the evening I invited him into my heart. What an entrance he made! It was not a spectacular, emotional thing, but very real, occurring at the very center of my soul. He came into the darkness of my heart and turned on the light. He built a fire in the cold hearth and banished the chill. He started music where there had been stillness and harmony where there had been discord. He filled the emptiness with his own loving fellowship. I have never regretted opening the door to Christ and I never will.

This, of course, is the first step in making the heart Christ's home. He has said, "Listen! I am standing at the door, knocking; if you hear my voice and open the door, I will come in to you and eat with you, and you with me" (Rev 3:20). If you want to know the reality of God and the personal presence of Jesus Christ at the innermost part of your being, simply open wide the door and ask him to come in and be your Savior and Lord.

After Christ entered my heart, in the joy of that new found relationship, I said to him, "Lord, I want this heart of mine to be yours. I want you to settle down here and be fully at home. I want you to use it as your own. Let me show you around and point out some of the features of the home so that you may be more comfortable. I want you to enjoy our time together." He was glad to come and seemed delighted to be given a place in my ordinary, little heart.

The Study

The Study

The first room we looked at together was the study — the library. Let us call it the study of the mind. Now in my home this room of the mind is a small room with thick walls. But it is an important room. In a sense, it is the control room of the house. He entered with me and looked around at the books in the bookcase, the magazines on the table, the pictures on the walls. As I followed his gaze, I became uncomfortable. Strangely enough, I had not felt badly about this room before, but now that he was there with me looking at these things, I was embarrassed. There were some books on the shelves his eyes were too pure to look at. On the table were a few magazines a Christian has no business reading. As for the pictures on the walls — the imaginations and thoughts of my mind — some of these were shameful.

Red-faced, I turned to him and said, "Master, I know this room really needs to be cleaned up and made over. Will you help me shape it up and change it to the way it ought to be?

"Certainly," he replied. "I'm glad to help you! I've come to handle things like this! First of all, take all the material you are reading and viewing which are not true, good, pure and helpful, and throw them out! Now put on the empty shelves the books of the Bible. Fill the library with the Scriptures and meditate on them day and night. As for the pictures on the walls, you will have difficulty controlling these images, but I have something that will help." He gave me a full-sized portrait of himself. "Hang this centrally," he said, "on the wall of the mind." I did, and I have discovered through the years that when my thoughts are centered on Christ, the awareness of his presence, purity and power causes wrong and impure thoughts to back away. So he has helped me to bring my thoughts under his control, but the struggle remains.

If you have difficulty with this little room of the mind, let me encourage you to bring Christ there. Pack it full with the Word of God, study it, meditate on it and keep clearly before you the presence of the Lord Jesus.

The Dining Room

The Dining Room

From the study we went into the dining room, the room of appetites and desires. Now this was a large room, a most important place to me. I spent a lot of time and hard work trying to satisfy all my wants.

I told him, "This is a favorite room. I'm sure you will be pleased with what we serve here."

He seated himself at the table and inquired, "What is on the menu for dinner tonight?"

"Well," I said, "my favorite dishes: money, academic degrees, stocks, with newspaper articles of fame and fortune as side dishes." These were the things I liked, thoroughly secular fare. There was nothing so very bad in any of them, but it was not really the kind of food which would feed the soul and satisfy true spiritual hunger.

When the plates were placed before my new friend, he said nothing. However, I observed that he did not eat. I asked, somewhat disturbed,

"Savior, don't you like this food? What is the trouble?"

He answered, "I have food to eat you do not know of. My food is to do the will of him that sent me." He looked at me again and said, "If you want food that really satisfies you, do the will of your heavenly Father. Put his pleasure before your own. Stop striving for your own desires, your own ambitions, your own satisfactions. Seek to please him. That food will really satisfy you. Try a bit of it!"

And there about the table he gave me a taste of doing God's will. What flavor! There is no food like it in all the world. It alone satisfies. At the end everything else leaves you hungry.

What's the menu in the dining room of our desires? What kind of food are we serving our divine companion and serving ourselves? "All that is in the world, the desire of the flesh and the desire of the eyes and the pride in riches" (1 Jn 2:16), our self-centered wants? Or are we finding God's will to be our soul-satisfying meat and drink?

The Living Room

The Living Room

We moved next into the living room. This was a quiet, comfortable room with a warm atmosphere. I liked it. It had a fireplace, sofa, overstuffed chairs, a bookcase and an intimate atmosphere.

He also seemed pleased with it. He said, "Indeed, this is a delightful room. Let's come here often. It's secluded and quiet, and we can have good talks and fellowship together."

Well, naturally, as a young Christian I was thrilled. I couldn't think of anything I would rather do than have a few minutes alone with Christ in close companionship.

He promised, "I will be here every morning early. Meet me here and we will start the day together."

So, morning after morning, I would go downstairs to the living room. He would take a book of the Bible from the bookcase, open it, and we would read it together. He would unfold to me the wonder of God's saving truth recorded on its pages and make my heart sing as he shared all he had done for me and would be to me. Those times together were wonderful. Through the Bible and his Holy Spirit he would talk to me. In prayer I would respond. So our friendship deepened in these quiet times of personal conversation.

However, under the pressure of many responsibilities, little by little, this time began to be shortened. Why, I'm not sure. Somehow I assumed I was just too busy to give special, regular time to be with Christ. This was not a deliberate decision, you understand; it just seemed to happen that way. Eventually not only was the period shortened, but I began to miss days now and then, such as during midterms or finals. Matters of urgency demanding my attention were continually crowding out the quiet times of conversation with Jesus. Often I would miss it two days in a row or more.

One morning, I recall rushing down the steps in a hurry to be on my way to an important appointment.

As I passed the living room, the door was open. Glancing in I saw a fire in the fireplace and Jesus sitting there. Suddenly, in dismay, it came to me, "He is my guest. I invited him into my heart! He has come as my Savior and Friend to live with me. Yet here I am neglecting him."

I stopped, turned and hesitantly went in. With downcast glance I said, "Master, I'm sorry! Have you been here every morning?"

"Yes," he said, "I told you I would be here to meet with you." I was even more ashamed! He had been faithful in spite of my faithlessness. I asked him to forgive me and he did, as he always does when we acknowledge our failures and want to do the right thing.

He said, "The trouble is that you have been thinking of the quiet time, of Bible study and prayer, as a means for your own spiritual growth. This is true, but you have forgotten that this time means something to me also. Remember, I love you. At a great cost I have redeemed you. I value your friendship. Just to have you look up into my face warms my heart. Don't neglect this hour if only for my sake. Whether or not you want to be with me, remember I want to be with you. I really love you!"

You know, the truth that Christ wants my fellowship, that he loves me, wants me to be with him and waits for me, has done more to transform my quiet time with God than any other single fact. Don't let Christ wait alone in the living room of your heart, but every day find a time and place when, with the Word of God and in prayer, you may be together with him.

The Workroom

The Workroom

Before long he asks, "Do you have a workroom in your house?"

Out in the garage of the home of my heart I had a workbench and some equipment, but I was not doing much with it. Once in a while I would play around at making a few little gadgets, but I wasn't producing anything substantial.

I took him out there.

He looked over the workbench and the few talents and skills I had. He said, "This is fairly well furnished. What are you producing with your life for the kingdom of God?" He looked at one or two of the little toys that I had thrown together on the bench and he held one up to me. "Is this the sort of thing you are doing for others in your Christian life?"

I felt terrible! "Lord, that's the best I can do. I know it isn't much. I'm ashamed to say that with my awkwardness and limited ability, I don't think I'll ever do much more."

"Would you like to do better?" he asked.

"You know I would!" I replied.

"Well, first remember what I taught you: 'Apart from me you can do nothing' (Jn 15:5)."

"Come, relax in me and let my Spirit work through you. I know you are unskilled, clumsy and awkward, but the Spirit is the Masterworker. If he controls your heart and your hands, he will work through you. Now turn around." Then putting his great strong arms around me and his hands under mine he picked up the tools and began to work through me. "Relax. You are still too tense. Let go — let me do the work!"

It amazes me what his skilled hands can do through mine if I only trust him and let him have his way. I am very far from satisfied with the product that is being turned out. I still get in his way at times. There's much more that I need to learn. But I do know that whatever has been produced for God has been through him and through the power of his Spirit in me.

Don't be discouraged because you cannot do much for God. It's not our ability but our availability that's important. Give what you are to Christ. Be sensitive and responsive to what he wants to do. Trust him. He will surprise you with what he can do through you!

The
Rec Room

The Rec Room

I remember the time he inquired about the rec room, where I went for fun and fellowship. I was hoping he would not ask me about that. There were certain associations and activities I wanted to keep for myself. I did not think Jesus would enjoy or approve of them. I evaded the question.

However, one evening when I was on my way out with some of my buddies for a night on the town, he was at the door and stopped me with a glance. "Are you going out?"

I answered, "Yes."

"Good," he said, "I would like to go with you."

"Oh," I replied rather awkwardly. "I don't think, Lord, that you would really enjoy where we are going. Let's go out together tomorrow night. Tomorrow night we can go to a Bible class or a social at the church, but tonight I have another engagement."

"As you wish," was his comment. "Only I thought when I came into your home we were going to do everything together — be close companions! Just know that I am willing to go with you!"

"Well," I said, "we'll go someplace together tomorrow night!"

That evening I spent some miserable hours. I felt rotten! What kind of a friend was I to Jesus? Deliberately leaving him out of part of my life, doing things and going places that I knew very well he would not enjoy? When I returned that evening, there was a light in his room and I went up to talk it over with him. I acknowledged, "Lord, I have learned my lesson. I know now I can't have a good time if you are not along. From now on we will do everything together!"

Then we went down together into the rec room of the house. He transformed it. He brought new friendships, new excitement, new joys. Laughter and music have been ringing in the house ever since. With a twinkle in his eye, he smiled, "You thought that with me around you wouldn't have much fun, didn't you? Remember, I have come 'that my joy may be in you, and that your joy may be complete' " (Jn 15:11).

The Bedroom

The Bedroom

One day when we were in my bedroom he asked me about the picture next to my bed.

"That's a picture of my girlfriend." I told him. Though I knew my relationship with my girlfriend was a good one, I felt funny talking to him about it. She and I were struggling with some issues and I didn't want to discuss them with him. I tried to change the subject.

But Jesus must have known what I was thinking. "You are beginning to question my teaching on sex, aren't you? That intercourse is only for those who are joined in the covenant of marriage? You're feeling I may be asking something unnatural if not impossible for you. You're afraid my will on this will limit the full enjoyment of life and love. Isn't that true?"

"Yes," I confessed.

"Then listen carefully to what I am saying," he continued. "I forbid adultery and premarital sex not because sex is bad but because it is good. Beyond the physical ecstasy it is a means of bonding two lives in deepening love. It has the creative power to bring human life into being. Sex is powerful. Used properly, sex has tremendous potential for good. Used improperly, it destroys the good. For this reason God intends it to be expressed only within the commitment of a loving life partnership. There is far more to love than just sex.

"Let me help you in your relationship with the opposite sex. If you should fail and feel shame and guilt, know I still love you and will remain with you. Talk to me about it! Acknowledge the wrong! Take steps to avoid it happening again! Rely on my strength to keep you from falling and to lead you into a relationship of love in marriage where two truly become one in me."

The Hall Closet

The Hall Closet

There's one more matter of crucial consequence I would like to share with you. One day I found him waiting for me at the front door. An arresting look was in his eye. As I entered, he said to me, "There's a peculiar odor in the house. Something must be dead around here. It's upstairs. I think it is in the hall closet."

As soon as he said this I knew what he was talking about. Indeed there was a small closet up there on the hall landing, just a few feet square. In that closet behind lock and key I had one or two little personal things I did not want anybody to know about. Certainly I did not want Christ to see them. They were dead and rotting things leftover from the old life — not wicked, but not right and good to have in a Christian life. Yet I loved them. I wanted them so much for myself I was really afraid to admit they were there. Reluctantly I went up the stairs with him and as we mounted, the odor became stronger and stronger. He pointed at the door and said, "It's in there! Some dead thing!"

It made me angry! That's the only way I can put it. I had given him access to the study, the dining room, the living room, the workroom, the rec room, the bedroom and now he was asking me about a little two-by-four closet. I said to myself, "This is too much! I am not going to give him the key."

"Well," he responded, reading my thoughts, "if you think I'm going to stay up here on the second floor with this smell, you are mistaken. I will take my bed out on the back porch or somewhere else. I'm certainly not going to stay around that." And I saw him start down the stairs.

When you have come to know and love Jesus Christ, one of the worst things that can happen is to sense him withdrawing his face and fellowship. I had to give in. "I'll give you the key," I said sadly, "but you'll have to open the closet and clean it out. I haven't the strength to do it."

"I know," he said. "I know you haven't. Just give me the key. Just authorize me to handle that closet and I will." So, with trembling fingers, I passed the key over to him. He took it from my hand, walked over to the door, opened it, entered it, took out the putrefying stuff that was rotting there and threw it all away. Then he cleansed the closet, painted it and fixed it up all in a moment's time. Immediately a fresh, fragrant breeze swept through the house. The whole atmosphere changed. What release and victory to have that dead thing out of my life! No matter what sin or what pain there might be in my past, Jesus is ready to forgive, to heal and to make whole.

Transferring
the Title

Transferring the Title

Then a thought came to me. I said to myself, "I have been trying to keep this heart of mine clean and available for Christ but it is hard work. I start on one room and no sooner have I cleaned it than I discover another room is dirty. I begin on the second room and the first one is already dusty again. I'm getting tired trying to maintain a clean heart and an obedient life. I just am not up to it!"

Suddenly I asked, "Lord, is there a possibility you would be willing to manage the whole house and operate it for me just as you did that closet? Could I give to you the responsibility of keeping my heart what it ought to be and myself doing what I ought to be doing?"

I could see his face light up as he replied, "I'd love to! This is exactly what I came to do. You can't live out the Christian life in your own strength. That is impossible. Let me do it for you and through you. That's the only way it will really work! But," he added slowly, "I am not the owner of this house. Remember, I'm here as your guest. I have no authority to take charge since the property is not mine."

In a flash it all became clear. Excitedly I exclaimed, "Lord, you have been my guest, and I have been trying to play the host. From now on you are going to be the owner and master of the house. I'm going to be the servant!"

Running as fast as I could to the strongbox, I took out the title deed to the house describing its assets and liabilities, its condition, location and situation. Then rushing back to him, I eagerly signed it over giving title to him alone for time and eternity. Dropping to my knees, I presented it to him, "Here it is, all that I am and have forever. Now you run the house. Let me stay with you as houseboy and friend."

He took my life that day and I can give you my word, there is no better way to live the Christian life. He knows how to keep it and use it. A deep peace settled down on my soul that has remained. I am his and he is mine forever!

*May Christ settle down and be at home
as Lord of your heart also.*